leopard gecko

understanding and
caring for your pet

Written by
Lance Jepson MA VetMB CBiol MSB MRCVS

leopard gecko

understanding and
caring for your pet

Written by
Lance Jepson MA VetMB CBiol MSB MRCVS

Magnet & Steel Ltd

www.magnetsteel.com

Printed and bound in China by Printworks Global Limited.

ISBN: 978-1-907337-17-8
ISBN: 1-907337-17-2

Contents

The leopard gecko

The leopard gecko (Eublepharis macularius) has become something of a reptile-keeping phenomenon. It is a small lizard that is highly adaptable to a life in captivity providing that its basic needs are met.

Leopard geckos have a docile personality, require relatively modest amounts of space and equipment and have a naturally attractive pattern of dark brown to black spots and squiggles on a yellow background (that is before one takes into account the myriad of colour morphs that are now being produced for the pet trade). Unlike the crested gecko, their colours and patterns alter little with the time of day.

The leopard gecko has something for everyone – it is the ideal first lizard for the novice reptile-keeper and yet, with its complex genetics and morphs, there is much to keep the advanced hobbyist interested.

Evolution

Leopard geckos belong to the Eublepharinae, which is one of the four sub-families of the gecko family Gekkonidae. It is an ancient lineage with representatives in Asia (Goniurosaurus, Aeluroscalabotes and Eublepharis species, the last of which includes our leopard gecko - E. macularius), sub-Saharan African species (Hemitheconyx and Holodactylus) and the North America/northern Central American representatives - Coleonyx species.

Geckos are first recorded in the fossil record in present-day Germany, dating from the late Jurassic, around 208 – 146 million years ago (Mya). It seems that Goniosaurus are the most primitive of the Eublepharine geckos, whilst the African species are the most recently evolved (Ota et al 1999). This argues that this group of geckos developed in Laurasia (the landmass that gave rise to both North America and Asia) and therefore they must have evolved somewhere between 200 Mya (when Laurasia was formed) and 60 Mya, the point at which Asia and North America went their separate ways. It is thought that there was a subsequent secondary invasion of eublepharine geckos from their homeland into Africa (via the Arabian plate, around 20 Mya), and presumably India (from 50 Mya), when these continents again connected with Asia.

Geographically, leopard gecko species are spread around the Iranian Plateau, but in a fairly erratic manner. It seems likely that their patchy distribution is linked to various geologic events, including the lifting of the Iranian Plateau during the Pliocene (5.3 to 2.5 Mya).

The Iranian Plateau is the area at the junction between the northward moving Arabian Plate and the Eurasian Plate. The distribution of the eastern leopard gecko E .hardwickii was at one point separated from that of E. macularius group by an extension of the Tethys Sea (of which the Mediterranean Sea is a remnant) during the mid-Miocene (23 to 5.3 Mya). This separation probably allowed speciation to occur from the E. macularius group, while today a large arid area continues to separate these species. It is therefore likely that the colliding of the various tectonic plates (Eurasia, Africa, Arabian, Indian) has caused recurring geologic upheavals, each of which could progressively isolate populations for sufficient lengths of time for different species to develop.

Species &
sub-species

Species & sub-species

Leopard geckos are part of a group of geckos known as the Eublepharinae. The name refers to their eyelids (Eu = true and blepharon = eyelid), but many people refer to them by another characteristic – the fat-tailed geckos. There are several species of leopard gecko.

The common leopard gecko (Eublepharis macularius macularius) is native to Asia, in particular Pakistan and Afghanistan but has also been described in the Caspian Area and Iraq. In Pakistan they are recorded from Rabwan, Chiniot, Lalian, Ahmadpur Sial and the Northwest Frontier Province. They are also present in Blauchistan, an area that was divided by the British colonists in three regions – part was annexed to Iraq, part to Afghanistan and the bulk to Pakistan.

A leopard gecko's eyelids give them their scientific name.

The Afghan leopard gecko (E. m. afghanicus) seems to be reasonably distinct and is native to south-east Afghanistan, primarily along the Kabul River area and the neighboring Pakistani North Eastern Provinces. These geckos are also found north of Kabul, especially around the towns of Gulbahar and Charikar. Their range extends as far as the Hindu Kush Mountains. Afghan leopard geckos are smaller than E. m.macularius, with males having a snout-vent length of around 10 cm. Females are slightly smaller.

The range of the leopard gecko was also said to include India and may still include the Khandesh District. Other stated areas included modern-day Rajasthan and western parts such as northern Karnataka, Maharashtra and Gujarat. Such Indian populations were distinguishable from the common leopard gecko and were initially designated as a separate subspecies (E. m. fuscus). This has now been elevated to the species status of E. fuscus (Das 1997). The area around Mumbai was the type locality for E. fuscus.

Although the founding leopard geckos for the pet trade came from Pakistan (probably from around Sind), De Vosjoli et al (2005) comment that the original group brought together in the USA by Ron

Tremper may have included geckos from India, indicating that many of the modern captive-bred leopard geckos in the pet trade may be *macularius x fuscus* hybrids.

However, the taxonomy of leopard geckos is in some confusion, with some authorities dividing the leopard gecko into a variable number of sub-species. The most western population in Pakistan is considered by some to be a different subspecies E. m. montanus, whilst others have further subdivided the leopard gecko into an array of sub-species including Eublepharus (macularius) fasciolatus, E. smithi and E. gracilis. Since the separation of these assorted sub-species is largely based on differences in colour pattern, it is equally likely that these could be just geographic races or variants.

Other Eublepharis species are the East Indian leopard gecko, the Iraqi Eyelid Gecko and the Turkmenistan Eyelid Gecko.

- East Indian Leopard Gecko, Indian Leopard Gecko or Indian Fat-tailed Gecko (E. hardwickii) is from north, central and eastern India, including Madhya Pradesh and probably Bangladesh.

- The Iraqi Eyelid Gecko, Western Leopard Gecko or Iranian Fat-tailed Gecko E. angramainyu is found in east- and west-central Iraq, western-central Iran, Turkey (Anatolia) and Syria (Zagros-Mountains). Males can have a snout-vent length of around 15 cm, with the tail a further 10 cm. The specific name is derived from the term 'Angra Mainyu' - the Zoroastrian 'Spirit of Darkness' - referring to the nocturnal nature of these lizards.

- The Turkestan Leopard Gecko, Turkmenian Fat-tailed Gecko or Turkmenistan Eyelid gecko E. turcmenicus is native to Turkmenistan and northern parts of Iran.

Eublepharis macularius is only one of several related species.

Natural history & ecology

Leopard geckos are natives of dry, rocky environments. The type specimen described by Blyth in 1854 was from the Salt Range, Punjab. Areas they have been found in include, hard clay soil covered with sand in areas where numerous Zygophyllum bushes where growing, on fairly open alluvial soils, in sandstone rocky areas and in rock wall crevices in Pakistan.

Throughout the daytime and during the colder months these geckos rest in rock crevices and under large stones where the local humidity can be quite high, and where the surrounding rocks, warmed by the daytime sun, provide an ideal thermal environment.

Khan (1972) details finding leopard geckos on the ground, under stones, in the Jhangh District of central Punjab, Pakistan – some 40 miles from the type locality of the Salt Range. Khan describes the area as having a semi-arid climate, with an annual rainfall of 7-12 inches (19 to 30 cm). Leopard geckos were present amongst the rocky hills in that area.

Khan and Tasnim (1990) mention collecting leopard geckos near Goi-Madan, south-western Azad Kashmir. They were associated with sandstone areas. In this area the hottest month is June when the temperature reaches 27 to 30°C (80.6 to 86°F), while in the winter sub-zero temperatures are recorded in January and February. Monsoon rains occur from June to mid-September, with July and August being the wettest months. Annual rainfall is 16-17 cm and snowfall frequently occurs during January or February.

Göçmen (2003) describes the Afghanistan subspecies E. m. afghanicus as living in rocky deserts and sparse grasslands on clay soil, yet avoiding sand. This sub-species, and probably the nominate E. m macularius, is found in large colonies. He describes them as being quite abundant from mid-April until late May and that they are also readily found until the end of August into September. It would therefore seem that locally these geckos are only active during the warmer times of the year. Göçmen further states that in the western foothills of the Zagros Mountains, the Western leopard gecko (E. angramainyu) was found readily on a few nights, again from mid-April until late May, and could be collected until late August. The geckos were readily observed on the roads at night, usually when the air temperatures were between 32°C (89.6°F) and 34.4°C (93.9°F) and the road surface temperatures were 32.6°C (90.7°F) to 36.4°C (97.5°F). The roads were at least 20°C (68°F) higher than the surrounding soil temperatures.

Leopard geckos have a preferred body temperature of 28 to 30°C (82.4 to 86°F).

Tangerine eclipse

They are primarily thigmotherms, gaining their body heat by direct contact with warm surfaces rather than basking directly in sunshine. This would explain their increased activity rates and hence observed presence during the warmest months of the year when night temperatures could support such behaviours. Therefore, it also seems that in the wild, leopard geckos will undergo brumation (also known as hibernation) during the coldest months of the year and conversely are at their most active from late spring into late summer.

Leopard geckos are unusual reptiles in that they select discrete areas to use as toilets. Known as defaecatoriums, these are communal areas where the leopard geckos will trek to urinate and defaecate. This may be an adaptation to a more colonial existence, drawing potential predators away from the main retreat areas and possibly limiting environmental contamination by internal parasites. They may also serve a social function, allowing individuals to monitor pheromones in other individuals that they may not necessarily have direct contact with. This may involve assessing who is around or whether anyone is sexually active. Defaecatoriums may also act as colony markers.

Wild Leopard geckos are only active during the warmest months of the year.

Diet

Leopard geckos are carnivores. In the wild their diet consists of anything that is available and small enough to be overpowered. Typically this includes a range of insects and other arthropods such as grasshoppers, beetles, spiders, scorpions and solpugids (sun spiders).

Predators

Leopard geckos are a handy-sized packet of protein and can fall victim to a variety of nocturnal predators including foxes, domestic dogs and cats, jackals, wolves and owls. The Soosan Tiger snake (Telescopus tessellatus), probably a lizard-eating snake, is also found in part of the range of leopard geckos. Leopard geckos are often found hunting on roads at night and many are killed by traffic.

Leopard gecko – beautiful pet to us, but a quick snack for its many predators!

References

Das, I. (1997). Resolution of the systematic status of Eublepharis macularius fuscus Borner, 1981 (Eublepharidae: Sauria: Squamata). Hamadryad 22(1): 13-20.

De Vosjoli, P., Tremper, R. and Klingenberg R. (2005) The Herpetoculture of Leopard Geckos. Advanced Visions Inc.

Göçmen, B. (2003) Leopard Geckos (Sauria: Eublepharidae) of the World - Eublepharis macularius (Blyth, 1954) http://sci.ege.edu.tr/~bgocmen/emacularius.html

Khan, M.S. (1972) Checklist and Key to the Lizards of Jhangh District, West Pakistan. Herpetologica. 28: (2) 94 – 98.

Khan, M.S. and Tasnim, R. (1990) A new gecko of the genus Tenuidactylus from Northeastern Punjab, Pakistan, and Southwestern Azad Kashmir. Herpetologia. 46 (2) 142-148

Ota, H. Honda, M. Kobayashi., M. Sengoku, S. and Hikida, T. (1999) Phylogenetic Relationships of Eublepharid Geckos (Reptilia: Squamata): A Molecular Approach. Zoological Science 16: 659–666

Anatomy & behaviour

The leopard gecko is generally a small lizard. Wild caught males have a snout-vent length (the distance from the tip of their nose to the cloaca) of 15 to 16 cm, with females slightly smaller at 14.5 to 15 cm. In the case of pet leopard geckos, most will have a total length (including the tail) of roughly 15 to 25 cm. Weight can vary from 50 to 60 g, although exceptionally large males can tip the scales at 100 g, whilst the genetic giant morphs will regularly reach 100 to 150 g and can have a total length of 29 cm.

Some large males can tip the scales at 100g.

The Leopard Gecko is a typical lizard shape, and appears quite stout. The jaw is relatively massive, which probably reflects the crunchiness of its natural diet. Just above and behind the corner of the mouth is the ear. There is no external ear flap or pinna – instead the tympanic scale, the equivalent of our ear drum, is exposed, although recessed slightly into the head.

In the centre, on the top of the head, is a small structure often called the pineal eye. This is a vestigial eye-like structure which is light sensitive and is thought to monitor light levels including periodicity and intensity. It is wired into the pineal gland, a structure in the brain that is involved with the setting and control of internal biological rhythms such as brumation, but also includes daily circadian rhythms.

Leopard gecko toes are short, cylindrical and are tipped with claws. The undersides carry transverse lamellae but they do not have the adhesive qualities that enable them to climb vertical walls like, for example, crested geckos (Rhacodactylus ciliatus). At the tops of the front legs are very pronounced armpits known as axial pockets. Their function, if they have one, is unknown. In well-fed leopard geckos there is often a small bulge of fat immediately behind the armpit.

The ears are obvious on leopard geckos.

The body is carried proud of the substrate in healthy leopard geckos. The tail is shorter than the head and body and in a healthy specimen is quite bulbous. Leopard geckos may not be able to climb sheer surfaces very well but, as a ground adapted lizard, they can run if necessary, and have been timed at speeds of up to 1 metre per second (Aerts et al 2000).

The skin is made up of small scales and on the back there are a number of larger tubercles. As part of their growth and skin maintenance leopard geckos will regularly shed their skins in a process known as ecdysis. The older outer layer of skin is spread in sheets, although you may not always know this has happened because a healthy leopard gecko will eat the shed skin. Although the reason for them doing this is unclear, it has been suggested that this is an anti-predator behaviour. Leaving shed skin lying around is likely to attract predators, especially snakes. By eating the sheds not only do leopard geckos remove the tell-tale skins from their immediate environment, but the use of defaecatoriums will deposit this material, once digested, some distance away from the individual and colony.

Healthy leopard geckos will shed their skin regularly.

It is the colouring and pattern of the wild geckos that give us the name leopard gecko. They possess a base colour of mid to bright yellow along the back and flanks, fading to a white underside. Superimposed on this is a complex pattern of brown to black spots which may join together to form squiggles and short lines. In hatchling leopard geckos the young are banded with large patches of colour alternating with the base colour. These gradually break up and fade until by around three months of age the pattern is more typical of the adult. Selective breeding has produced a rainbow of colours and patterning, yet the original wild gecko, with its spotted marking, still retains a certain beauty.

Unlike most species of gecko, leopard geckos have well-developed, functioning upper and lower eyelids. These eyelids are sufficiently unusual to give this whole group their name, and the leopard geckos bear the generic name of Eublepharius, which roughly translated from its Ancient Greek origins means true eyelids. The pupil is a vertical slit during the day but is able to expand to cover almost the entire eye during the hours of darkness to maximise light penetration to the retina. Leopard gecko vision is good and sight is probably their main sense. Their colour vision is also good and it is thought that leopard geckos can see in the ultraviolet spectrum.

Leopard geckos have two ears that are set well back on the head, and have reasonably good hearing.

They have three means of sensing food and other chemicals. These are olfaction (sense of smell) detected in the lining of the nose; gustation (taste) detected in the lining of the tongue and other oral surfaces; vomerolfaction detected in the lining of specialised vomeronasal organs situated in the roof of the mouth. Vomerolfaction picks up non-airbourne scent particles from the tongue and lining of the mouth and may play a part not only in food detection, but also individual recognition based on an individual's scent profile. This may apply as much to how your gecko recognises you, as it does to how it tells other leopard geckos apart.

Leopard geckos can autotomise, or shed, their tail. This is a common anti-predation adaptation seen in many gecko and other lizard species, but is particularly well developed in leopard geckos. The tail detaches from the body close to its base, where there are specific separation points in the tail vertebrae, the muscles and the blood vessels so that there is a minimum amount of blood loss and trauma to the gecko.

The site of the break is usually at the level of the sixth caudal (tail) vertebra. Once separated the tail muscles engage in erratic spasmodic movements for some time after detachment. These erratic movements consists of rhythmic swinging backwards and forwards with occasional jumps, lunges and even flips up to 3 cm in height! This is highly attractive to predators and is used as a distraction to lure attention away from the gecko. The rocky terrain in which leopard geckos evolved lends itself to such tail acrobatics, and these can last up to thirty minutes. Shedding the tail may also lighten the gecko so that it can run faster. The tail will regrow given time, although its shape and pattern will be different from the original. The scales on a regenerated tail are circular and slightly convex. For a leopard gecko, autotomy is a last-ditch attempt to save it's life, so should it happen the chances are that the gecko is very stressed indeed.

Reptiles excrete their metabolic waste nitrogen not as urea as we do, but as uric acid crystals – the white sand-like sludgy substance naturally present in their urine. Note that this is not calcium as many people believe.

Young, immature geckos are difficult to sex.

Reptiles attempt to save water and by excreting uric acid as a sludge they avoid wasting water as urine rather than by eliminating nitrogen as urea. Urea is a substance that requires relatively large volumes of water in which to be dissolved and transported. The kidneys are paired structures situated close to the pelvis. Urine is formed in the kidneys and is drained down the ureters (tubes that connect the kidneys to the bladder) where it is stored. Unfortunately reptile kidneys cannot concentrate urine, so this is further concentrated by having water absorbed from it across the bladder wall or by refluxing it back into the large intestine.

As with all reptiles, leopard geckos do not have separate external orifices for the urinogenital tract and bowel; instead they have a cloaca which is a chamber into which the gut, bladder and reproductive tract all communicate. This intermingling of excreta is largely why leopard geckos often produce urine and faeces at the same time. The entrance to the cloaca is ventrally at the base of the tail and the entrance is marked by a slit-like opening.

Females possess two ovaries. On each ovary a follicle will develop, from which an egg is ultimately produced.

Hemipenal bulges and preanal pores are obvious in adult males (bottom) and absent or minimal in females (top).

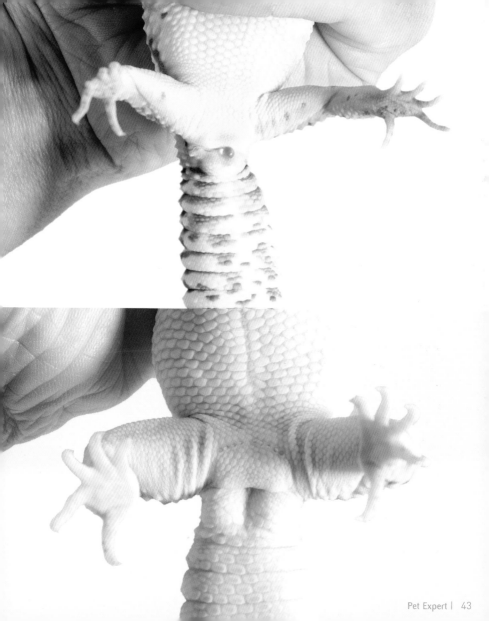

At the stage of ovulation the follicle looks like an egg-yolk and will pass into the oviduct where the shell membrane and the shell itself are subsequently laid down. The follicles and eggs are so large that can be seen through the skin of the underside of the gecko. A normal clutch is two eggs.

Male leopard geckos have two testes that lie internally. They do not possess a true penis but instead have two structures called hemipenes. These are found behind the cloaca at the base of the tail and in mature males two swellings, the hemipenal bulges, mark their position. These bumps are therefore not the testes as many people believe. Only one hemipene is used at a time during mating, and it may occasionally be seen protruding immediately following a mating. This is usually nothing to worry about as normally it will retract on its own. The hemipenes play no part in urination. In front of the cloaca are the preanal pores, arranged in a V-shape. These pores are thought to produce sex-related pheromones and are relatively pronounced in sexually mature males compared with females. When used, the gecko will press these against the surface to be scent marked and rub them from side to side. This enlargement of the pores is a secondary sexual characteristic and, like beards in men, will only develop properly after sexual maturity. Using these to sex immatures and hatchlings with the aid of an ocular loupe is unlikely to be successful (but you do have a 50:50 chance).

The differences are best summed up in table form:

CHARACTERISTIC	MALE	FEMALE
HEMIPENAL BULGE	Adult males very obvious behind the cloaca and on the underside of the tail. Gently raising the tail may exaggerate the bulges. Immatures: not very obvious. No obvious bulges.	No obvious bulges.
PREANAL PORES	Very pronounced, often slightly proud of the skin. Immatures: only noticeable as dots at the preanal regions.	Not very pronounced. Appear as small circles with a central dot. Immatures: only noticeable as dots at the preanal regions.
HEAD & NECK SIZE	Head is wider and more robust, and the neck is thicker in adult males.	Head is narrower, more pointed towards the nose and less robust. Neck is slimmer.

Lifespan

Leopard geckos can be long-lived lizards and can survive well into their teens. Exceptional individuals have even survived to over twenty years old, putting them on par with the family cat for longevity. Most adult females are reproductively active until around the age of eight, after which egg production becomes more erratic.

Behaviour

Leopard geckos are social animals that are found in groups in the wild. Individual leopard geckos are able to recognise, and discriminate between, other leopard geckos (LaDage 2007).

In captivity, and probably in the wild, males maintain a territory within which a number of females reside. Males are the larger sex and are more robust than females, with stouter heads and larger jaws. They also possess more pronounced preanal and femoral pores. Both of these differences from females are thought to be linked to male-male aggression, with the relatively large heads and massive jaws used as weapons and the femoral pores secreting pheromones which act as territorial markers. Adults males will fight and can bite each other viciously, putting those powerful jaws to good use.

Leopard geckos can be quite adventurous given the opportunity.

Feeding behaviour

Leopard geckos are carnivores and have two main types of feeding behaviour. Unlike many geckos they are active predators rather than ambush specialists and will track down live insects by sight.

Once a prey target is spotted, a leopard gecko will initially stalk it, lifting first one leg, pausing, and then lifting the next as it slowly closes in. Often the tail will swing slowly from side to side. This tail movement changes to a rapid vibration a split second the gocko lunges forward, moving in quickly to grab hold of the insect or other prey, before ingesting it whole. Larger prey items may be shaken vigorously. However leopard geckos have an alternative, much more cautious strategy, sometimes they will approach foods slowly and will lick them first.

Good eyesight, even at night, helps a leopard gecko find its food.

By doing this they gain information on the potential food using vomerolfaction. At the tip of the tongue is an area which has papillae that are very different from those of the other tongue regions. These papillae are modified to enhance the gathering and transportation of fluid from the gecko's surrounding and transfer it to the vomeronasal organ. Not only does this mean that the leopard gecko can detect food that is not moving, but it may allow the gecko to track prey that it cannot see.

Vocalisation

Leopard geckos have a voice, it's not a loud one, but it is there. Usually the most that is heard is a chirping or clicking when the gecko is unhappy, for example if being handled.

Leopard geckos may vocalise when handled.

Sexual behaviour

Courtship in leopard geckos is usually initiated by the male. He will approach a female, and while doing so he may lick the substrate, or the air, eventually licking the female. The skin of a sexually active female contains an attractivity pheromone which triggers an amorous response in the male – he vibrates his tail rapidly to create an audible buzz and a vibration that the female can feel. A female which is ready to mate, will signal this by remaining still and lifting her tail. The male will then mount the female, simultaneously gripping her skin in his jaws, and mating occurs.

Females can be kept in pairs or more.

Effects of temperature

Leopard geckos are ectotherms – in other words they are dependant upon external heat sources to fuel their metabolism (cold-blooded is another term occasionally used but with a preferred body temperature of 28 to 30°C (82.4 to 86°F), it's not so cold!). They are behavioural thermoregulators (i.e. they alter their behaviour to adjust their body temperature) and they do this primarily by favouring localised warm environments, including heated surfaces.

Leopard geckos enjoy warm surfaces.

Leopard geckos, as nocturnal lizards, will rarely
bask under either real, or artificial, sunlight.
Keeping at the correct body temperature is vitally
important as this supports the whole range of
chemical reactions and bodily functions, such as
food digestion, that keep the gecko alive.

Surprisingly, one of the most crucial and far ranging
effects that temperature can have on Leopard
Geckos is while they are still in the egg. Obviously
excessively high and low temperatures will cause the
death of the unborn embryo, but within the correct
incubation temperature range there can be some
startling effects. The most well known of these is
Temperature Dependant Sex Determination (TDSD).
The temperature at which the embryo is incubated
for the first 21 days or so, determines its sex. In
addition, both the incubation temperature and the
sex of the embryo affect the levels of sex hormones
in the developing lizard to such and extent that
profound changes can occur in the appearance and
the behaviour of the gecko.

Incubation of leopard gecko eggs at 26°C (78.8°F)
produces only females. At 30°C (86°F) most of the
hatching geckos are female (around 30% male to 70%
female). Increasing this to 32.5°C (90.5°F) reverses
that ratio to 70% males and 30% females but at 34°C
(93.2°F) virtually all the geckos are again female.

But the fun doesn't stop there. Males hatching from female biased temperatures (30°C [86°F]) are more sexually active, but less aggressive to females than those males incubated at a male-selecting 32.5°C (90.5°F). That first group of males has higher oestrogen (female hormone) and lower testosterone (male hormone) levels than the more macho male-biased incubated males. Those macho males also scent mark with the femoral and preanal pores more than the other group of males. The temperature effect is not just on the males however, high temperature females are more aggressive than lower temperature females, and are more masculine in appearance with broader heads, more obvious preanal pores and larger body size. They also lay less fertile eggs, this may be an effect of incubation temperature on their reproductive tract or it may be that their relatively increased aggression affects the mating process! Both high temperature and low temperature females lay less fertile eggs than those incubated at a female-biased 30°C (86°F).

Incubation does not just affect temperature and physique – it can also affect colour. To be specific it appears to have an effect on the production of the black pigment, melanin.

Muted colours and a grey cast indicate this gecko will shed its skin soon.

Sibling geckos incubated at different temperatures can appear markedly different – those incubated at 27°C (80.6°F)appear darker than those incubated at 34°C (93.2°F). It seems that exposing albino embryos to temperatures below 27°C (80.6°F) for longer than 24 hours will cause this effect. Full siblings incubated at 32°C (89.6°F) will often have little or no marking (de Vosjoli et al 2005). Whether this is a true direct temperature effect or is indirectly mediated by the sex hormones, especially testosterone, is uncertain. Lavender albinos are also a product of incubation temperature, turning up when eggs are incubated at 29.5 to 30.5°C (85.1 to 86.9°F).

References

Aerts P., van Damme, R. Vanhooydonck, B. Zaaf, A., and Herrel A. (2000) Lizard Locomotion: How Morphology meets Ecology Netherlands Journal of Zoology. 50 (2): 261-277

De Vosjoli, P., Tremper, R. and Klingenberg R. (2005) The Herpetoculture of Leopard Geckos. Advanced Visions Inc.

LaDage, L.P. (2007) The socio-sexual behaviors of the leopard gecko (Eublepharis macularius) Dissertation. The University of Memphis, 2007, 91 pages; AAT 3276716

Temperature Dependant Sex Determination makes leopard geckos complex indeed!

Buying a leopard gecko

Sources of leopard geckos

Leopard geckos deserve our very best care, and part of that is preparing yourself for your new arrival. Buying this book is an important first step as reading about them is vital in order to understand and care for them. Learn what you can of their care and requirements so that there are no surprises, financial or otherwise. Once you are happy that you can care for a leopard gecko properly, one of the most exciting parts of leopard gecko keeping awaits – purchasing your new companion.

There are several ways of obtaining a new Leopard Gecko, each of which has its own pros and cons.

Most good reptile pet shops will have a variety of healthy leopard geckos to choose from.

Pet shop

This is the most obvious source of a new pet Leopard
Gecko, but there is a wide variation in the quality of
geckos and the service that you receive. Pointers
towards a good shop are:

1. The obvious health of the leopard gecko (see
   later this chapter). This can be difficult to judge
   because leopard geckos often do not display well
   in shop vivaria. Inevitably they will be found behind
   or under vivarium furniture, especially any hides
   that may have been provided. Always ask for a
   look at the gecko. When handled they should be
   bright and alert (although they may initially try to
   get away from you). Leopard geckos that appear
   lethargic, non-responsive, thin or unwilling to
   open their eyes should be avoided. Always ask
   for a closer look at the gecko and, if safe to do so
   without dropping it or it escaping, handle it.

2. The provision of correct housing. This should be
   reasonably clean with minimal faecal soiling of
   the substrate and cage furniture. There should be
   no overcrowding or mixing of species. Hatchling
   baby geckos are often kept individually, on paper,
   in smaller containers within a heated cabinet.
   Minimum requirements should be a water bowl,
   feed bowl and a hide.

Remember that a shop vivarium setup is different from yours at home – it is not expected that the gecko will live out its lifetime in the shop so the priorities are that it needs to be readily cleanable and the gecko easily caught, so a more minimalist approach is often better.

3. The shop should have plenty of ancillary equipment available for purchase including lights, vivaria, substrate and nutritional supplements. Books and other helpful literature should also be available.

4. Knowledgeable staff.

If all of the boxes above are ticked it's probably a good place from which to buy your gecko.

Blood hypo

Internet

Purchasing a leopard gecko via the Internet might seem attractive, especially as the prices are often lower and there is often a greater range of colour morphs available than in the high street shops. You are, however, buying these leopard geckos unseen – both the gecko and level of care – and there is a significant risk involved. Seriously ill leopard geckos may be sold to unsuspecting buyers by unscrupulous suppliers, so beware. Run an Internet search on the company or breeder you are considering buying from to see if there are any comments, good or bad, about them. Regulations govern the transport of all vertebrate animals so if you cannot collect in person – which is the ideal - your leopard gecko should be shipped to you by an approved courier and not, as sometimes happens, via parcel post.

Private breeder

Buying from a private breeder should mean that you get an opportunity to assess the health of the leopard gecko as well as see its parents and the environment it was reared in. The quality of your leopard gecko will depend upon that of the breeder.

Reptile rescue and welfare organizations

It may be that some reptile rescue organizations have unwanted leopard geckos available for rehoming or sale. These will have been assessed by knowledgeable individuals and there will be a significant backup in terms of expertise. Such geckos may not be perfect however and frequently have a history of poor health and care.

Private sale

A significant number of leopard geckos are bought from private homes or acquaintances. This is the least safe means of acquiring a new leopard gecko.

How to spot a healthy leopard gecko

Leopard geckos are nocturnal so the chances are that when you go to buy your gecko, it will be sleeping. Once awake they are usually bright, alert and inquisitive. Some leopard geckos do not mind being picked up by strangers but others will attempt to escape. This is natural behaviour and at your first meeting you should not read too much into this. Hatchling and young leopard geckos are very likely to try to escape from being handled as this is instinctive anti-predator behaviour.

Bright eyes and alert posture suggests a healthy leopard gecko.

Handling

Always ask to examine your leopard gecko first, and either handle it yourself or, if you are worried about it escaping (or injuring itself), ask either someone competent to do it or have it persuaded into a clear container so that you can safely give it the once over.

One thing everyone worries about is autotomy – the shedding of the gecko's tail. The good news is that this very rarely occurs - the gecko has to be in a life-or-death situation (as judged by the gecko) or extremely ill before this happens. But please be restrained. Just because you know that you are not going to eat the gecko does not mean that he knows that!

Leopard geckos that have been handled well can be easily encouraged on to the hand. Keep your palm slightly cupped with the gecko's head pointed towards the top of your hand. This allows some control over the gecko. Should it decide to start wandering, place your other hand, palm upwards, in front of the gecko such that it walks from your first hand on to the second.

Position the leopard gecko so that it's head is towards the top, or leading edge, of your hand.

By constantly changing hands the gecko can move and explore without the risk of it being constrained and panicking. If allowed to walk the gecko is also less likely to jump. While on the hand many geckos will 'taste' your skin with their tongue, using their vomerolfaction to gain more information about you. They may even learn to recognise you this way!

Some geckos are nervous or are not used to being handled. They will object strongly if picked up against their will. Typically if restrained in the hand such geckos will attempt to escape, first by attempting to run or jump. If this fails then they may begin to swing their head and shoulders from side to side and, as a last resort, will attempt to bite. Their jaws are not strong however and a bite from a Leopard Gecko is more likely to be a shock than cause any damage. Such geckos are also likely to defaecate and urinate as well – possibly again as a 'surprise tactic' or maybe as a result of anxiety. Anxious geckos are best held in a more tightly cupped hand with the head held between the outer edge of your index finger and thumb pressed lightly, but firmly, on to the widest point of the skull. The cupped fingers restrict the movement of the gecko, but do not grip or crush the body of the gecko, because this can easily cause bruising or serious injury.

Give the leopard gecko a general once-over. Leopard
geckos, like most animals, are symmetrical so
any obvious deviation away from this should be
investigated. Healthy leopard geckos are often quite
robust in appearance and the tail should be thick
almost to the point of being bulbous. Well-fed animals
may have small fatty lumps in their axillae (armpits).
They should walk with their body lifted off the ground.
The eyes should be open and bright. Missing toes and
tail tips are often as a result of problems with skin
shedding. Lumps and bumps are likely to be abscesses
or possibly tumours. Those with shrunken tails and
thin bodies should be avoided at all costs – they may

just look undernourished, but could be carrying cryptosporidum. Regrown tails may look stubby, without the normal pattern, but is of no consequence to an otherwise healthy gecko.

Sexing is fairly straightforward for adults – look for the hemipenal bulges (just behind the cloaca) and pronounced preanal and femoral pores in males. Sexing hatchlings and immatures is difficult however, even with the use of an ocular loupe.

Where possible have a fresh faecal sample checked by your veterinarian as soon as possible, as intestinal parasites such as flagellates and worms are common.

A healthy leopard gecko will appear alert, hold its body well and have a reasonably thickened tail.

Colour
morphs

The wild-type leopard gecko is a beautiful animal, with a yellow background colouring, overlaid with a complex spotting and lines in black or dark brown. Leopard gecko skin contains three types of pigment-containing cells, and it is variations in the numbers, distribution and quality of these cells that produce the different colour morphs.

These cells are:

- **Melanophores.** These contain black pigment (melanin).

- **Xanthophores.** These carry red, yellow or orange pigment.

- **Iridophores.** These contain crystalline materials that reflect and refract light.

In the last ten years or so, selective breeding has allowed the development of a huge number of colour morphs, and at least one physical morph – the genetic giant. The naming of the various colour morphs is often part descriptive, part reference to whoever developed that morph, and part flight of fancy. Acronyms and word contractions are popular too! However, I would argue that, to date, all Leopard gecko morphs (apart from the original wild-type) fall into one of five different trait groups.

These groups are:

1. Altered Patterning

2. Reduced Black Pigmentation

3. Altered Colouring

4. Eye (iris) colouring

5. Physical

Some of these traits can be combined in the same gecko, which gives a sixth group of combinations. These multi-trait geckos are often quite stunning, and are frequently marketed as 'designer morphs', reflecting both their desirability and their high cost.

Altered patterning

The genes that control this set of traits alter
the presence or the distribution of the pigment-
containing cells, which in turn changes the
appearance of the markings.

Blizzards

These are patternless, with an overall background
colour of white to yellow, although typically they are a
greyish colour. Yellow blizzards are sometimes referred
to as 'Banana Blizzards'. This is a recessive gene.

Blizzards

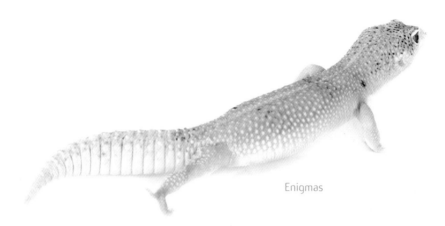

Enigmas

Enigmas

Enigmas are a difficult pattern to nail (hence the name!). When newly hatched the young have a blotched pattern rather than bands, and the tails are almost white. As they age the blotches increase and may form into a more speckled pattern. There are problems with some lines of Enigmas displaying neurological signs including circling and increased light sensitivity. Some may have prodigeous appetites and grow extremely fast. This is a dominant trait. Further to this, all engimas appear to be heterozygous (having only one copy of the gene) which suggests, although it is as yet unproven, that the homozygous form may be lethal, possibly causing early embryonic death.

Hypomelanistic

Often referred to as 'hypos', the gene for these alters the distribution of the black markings so that these geckos have only a very small number of black markings on the body, but there are still markings on the head and tail. 'Super-hypomelanistics' (super-hypos) have no body or head markings at all, frequently in combination with an orange body. In contrast 'baldies' is a term used more often in the USA for super-hypomelanistics, with no markings on the head or the body.

Jungle Albino

Jungle

Jungle leopard geckos have irregular markings that can form stripes, blotches or a marble-like pattern.

Murphy patternless

These geckos hatch with a full set of spots that gradually fade and disappear by 10 to 12 months of age. The eyes are normal. The colour can vary between daytime and nighttime. This is a recessive trait.

Patternless

These leopard geckos lack the typical spotted markings.

Patternless Albino

Patternless Mack Super Snow

Snow

The best specimen Snows
lack any of the background
yellow pigment, giving a high
contrast black on white pattern.
Technically these are axanthic
(lacking yellow pigment). 'Mack
Super Snows' have this high contrast pattern,
plus black eyes. Those geckos carrying
only one 'super snow' gene do not have the
black eyes and are known as 'Mack snows'.
It therefore shows incomplete dominance, only
expressing itself fully, with the black eyes, when in the
homozygous form (which has two copies of the gene,
one from each parent).

Mack Snow

Striped

Striped morphs have a band of light colour, typically edged with a darker, contrasting colour that extends along the mid-line of the back from the base of the neck to the base of the tail. Reversed striped morphs have a dark band outlined on either side by a lighter colour.

Redstripe

Standard Strip

Reduced black pigmentation

This does not mean fewer spots – the spots are
still there, but they are not visible because the
melanophores found there cannot synthesise any
black pigment. Animals that cannot produce the
pigment melanin (which can be black or brown)
because they lack the essential enzyme tyrosinase,
are usually termed albinos. This can be considered
as much a disorder as a colour trait. In leopard
geckos, however, it appears they are not true
albinos, but extreme amelanistics (failing to express
any black pigment). In other words, they produce
virtually no melanin, but still have the potential
capability to do so. Confused? It seems that all
strains have tyrosinase and in addition, under certain
(cooler) incubation conditions, brown-spotted or
lavender albinos can be produced. This condition
does not affect the red, yellow and orange pigment
cells, and in truth the lack of any melanophores to
mask these other colours can create stunningly-
coloured individuals, with bright white undersides,
vibrant yellow backs and orangey-yellow markings.

Rainwater Albino

Albinos

Three different strains of albino leopard gecko are known. These are the Tremper, Rainwater (Las Vegas) and Bell lines. Each of these is a recessive gene so that, for example, if you cross Tremper to Tremper, all the offspring will be albino. However if you cross between lines e.g. Tremper to Rainwater, all the young will be normally coloured. This suggests that in each line a different step in the biochemical pathway for melanin production is affected. The eyes of albinos are rarely true red or pink. Iris pigment is still present, although reduced in concentration.

Altered colouring

This group of morphs display altered colouring. This may be due to an increase in certain pigment-carrying cells, for example, high numbers of melanophores creating black-looking geckos, or new colours such as green or lavender. Some of these new colours may be due to changes in how the iridophores refract light.

Black

Until recently it was thought that no true jet black
leopard geckos had been produced. There were
melanistic strains of geckos that were predominantly
black, and as they matured the background colour
turned a dark yellow. However, it seems that some
breeders are working on true black strains under
such names as 'Black Velvet' and 'Black Pearl'.

Carrot-tails & carrot-heads

These are pretty much what it says on the tin. They
have heightened levels of orange pigmentation on
the tail (carrot-tail) or head (carrot-head).

Tangerine
Carrot Tail

Emeralds

These leopard geckos have patches of greenish colouration. New morphs such as Emerine (combining Emerald and Tangerine) are now being produced.

Yellow abyssinian

High-yellow

In these leopards the yellow colour is particularly bright and vivid. It can occur with any pattern (although they often have a reduced pattern) or none at all. Other names for this type include 'hyper-xanthic' or 'super yellow'.

Lavender

Leopard Geckos showing purple colouring on the body are classed as lavender. In some lines it is genetic, but can also be produced by incubating the eggs at 29.5 to 30.5°C (85.1 to 86.9°F).

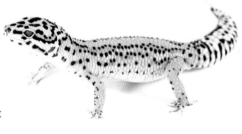

Lavender Stripe

Tangerine

Also known as orange, these geckos have high levels of orangey pigmentation on the body.

Tangerine

Eye colouring

Pigmentation of the iris can be quite variable.

There are two different genes for black eyes and one for red eye. A true red eye is only seen in the RAPTOR morph (see Designer Morphs below) and is a simple recessive. Those geckos of any colour and pattern with black eyes are known as 'Eclipse', and the gene for this eye colour is a recessive gene. The black eye in the Mack Super Snow (see Designer Morphs) behaves differently and is said to be co-dominant. Some Eclipse individuals exhibit eyes that are split 50:50 black and red, the colours separated by the pupil. These are sometimes referred to as 'snake eyes'.

Physical morphs

To date only one physical morph has been produced
– the genetic giant. These geckos grow considerably
larger than the normal leopard gecko – up to a total
length of 29 cm in males and weighing in at 100
to 150 g. Often said to be co-dominant, this trait
actually shows incomplete dominance. The usual
story is that 'giants' - those geckos which have only
one giant gene (i.e. from one parent) are larger than
a normal Leopard Gecko, while 'Super giants' (which
carry two sets of the gene, one from each parent),
can be larger still. Reality seems slightly different
and not all offspring are giant, nor are super giants
always bigger than giants. This may reflect the
degree of penetrance of the gene or even suggest
that other genes are involved. Environment plays a
part too – delayed breeding or individual rearing may
enhance the eventual adult size. This trait can be
combined with any of the colour morphs.

Young Giant

Combinations or designer morphs

The designer morphs are a group of leopard gecko lines that often exhibit a combination of traits and are valued as much for their rarity as their appearance. There is a constantly-expanding range of these, and here I have listed some of the more common ones, and one or two more interesting morphs.

A.P.T.O.R.

APTOR is an acronym for Albino Patternless Tremper Orange. These patternless albinos, often incorporating tangerine and super-hypomelanistic colourings, can be stunningly bright orange or yellow individuals.

Blazing Blizzards

These carry both the genes for Blizzard and those of an albino strain. The best ones have a pure white body, because the overall colouring (be it white or yellow), is enhanced by the removal of any black pigment cells. The albino genes can also give them red eyes, although black eyes are not unknown. Blazing Blizzards may also have 'snake eyes'.

creamsicle

Creamsicle

The Creamsicle is named after the frozen dessert of vanilla ice cream surrounded by orange-flavoured ice. They have orange or yellow blotches set on a white background. Genetically they are super-hypomelanistic, tangerine, carrot-tailed, Mack Snows.

dreamsicle

Dreamsickle

These are white with yellow spots combined with red eyes. They were produced from RAPTOR, Mack Snow and Enigma traits.

Raptor

Hybino

Hybino

These geckos are a brilliantly-intense orange colour.
This group includes the 'Sunglow' line developed
by Urban Geckos. These are actually albino, super-
hypomelanistic, carrot-tailed geckos.

Raptor

R.A.P.T.O.R.

Same morph as the APTOR, only this time combined
with the Ruby-eyed trait – hence 'RAPTOR'. As the
red (or ruby) eye defines a RAPTOR, this trait is a
simple recessive gene.

Caring for leopard geckos

The correct housing, possibly more than any other factor within our control, will govern how well we can look after our leopard geckos.

Previously we have looked at some aspects of a leopard gecko's natural history and how important parameters such as temperature and humidity are to these lizards. These vital needs must be addressed, a Leopard Gecko will not 'adapt' to a life if these are not correct; instead, it will eventually become ill and die.

Many families have only one leopard gecko. Geckos are not particularly sociable and males are territorial, so keeping a single individual will cause it no hardship.

Leopard geckos can climb reasonably well.

However, the variety of colours available, their ease of breeding and the fact that they can be kept in correctly-structured groups, means that many Leopard Gecko owners soon end up with a collection of Leopard Geckos! In view of that, here are some general recommendations on keeping groups of Leopard Geckos together:

1. Never mix leopard geckos with other species. They have fairly specific environmental parameters and if these are not provided then they will eventually become unwell; there is also a risk of disease cross-contamination. Leopard geckos are carnivorous and may eat smaller lizards of any species. This rule can be bent if the vivarium is large enough, the other inhabitants need a similar environment and no one is too small to be consumed, but most of the vivaria available to hobbyists are not suitable for this.

2. Keep one male to a vivarium.

3. Females and immatures can, in general, be kept in groups without too much aggression.

4. In mixed sex groups, a minimum ratio of 1:2 males to females is recommended, with preferably even more females. Some male leopard geckos are over amorous and this spreads out the attention of the male over several females, so that no one female has to endure his advances alone.

5. Hatchlings and young can be kept together, but watch out for bullying. Some individuals will eat most of the food, causing others to starve, plus twitching toes and tails may be accidently mistaken for live prey.

It's the sex ratios that matter with leopard gecko groups, not the patterns.

Checklist for the Minimum Equipment that you will need for your leopard gecko.

[✓] Pet Expert: Leopard gecko book

[✓] Vivarium

[✓] Heat lamp/ceramic bulb/heat mat

[✓] Thermostat

[✓] Thermometers x 2 (minimum)

[✓] Timer

[✓] Substrate

[✓] Furniture (e.g rocks)

[✓] Water bowl

[✓] Food bowl

[✓] Optional, but recommended: full spectrum light (2% UVB output)

Leopard geckos deserve our best care.

Vivaria

Vivaria are enclosed, often rectangular indoor housings that come in a variety of different materials and styles. Commercial breeders will use a rack system where individual or breeding groups of geckos are kept in multiple drawer-like containers. These work well for the geckos as they are in darkened, small to medium-sized spaces that mimic the animals' natural refuges. They also work well for the breeder because large numbers can be maintained in a relatively small area with chores such as cleaning and feeding rationalized for efficient use of time and space.

However, most of us home hobbyists want to see our geckos and give them a naturalistic and stimulating environment – a piece of their Pakistan desert in our own living room. For leopard geckos surface area is important and an absolute minimum vivarium would be 45 cm by 30 cm base, but the larger the better.

The simplest and least desirable of vivaria are those based on an aquarium or fish tank. Although easy to find, they have poor, top-only ventilation and access that makes them unsuitable. This therefore, can also make cleaning difficult.

Proper reptile vivaria are much better for captive leopard geckos. They are made from many different substances including wood, MDF, plastics and glass that can either be bought ready-made, as flat packs, or even built from scratch. The potential size and scope of a vivarium is limited only by the available space and the depth of your wallet.

Key features of a good vivarium are:

1. Access is via lockable sliding doors at the front of the vivarium. This greatly simplifies routine maintenance.

2. Water proofing. Leopard geckos need a dry environment, but urine and spilled water can lead to rotting wood, unless the joints are silicone sealed. If doing this yourself, use a sealer designed for aquaria, rather than bathroom sealants that contain potentially toxic fungicides.

3. Ventilation is crucial to the well-being of leopard geckos. Normally ventilation is achieved by installing grids of mesh or plastic at opposite ends of the vivarium. These grids are positioned at different heights so that as warm air rises it exits from the higher ventilation panel while fresh air is drawn in through the lower. Some of the modern glass vivaria have mesh lids which, when combined with side-opening grills, greatly enhance airflow. There are also small fans available, which can either be connected to a timer or better still to a thermostat so that they are switched on when the temperature in the vivarium becomes too high.

4. With glass vivaria, opaque strips may need to be placed along the bottom of the sides to provide a visual barrier that the leopard gecko can perceive.

Perhaps the most difficult aspect of keeping leopard geckos (and other reptiles) in vivaria is how to recreate the sun in the box. This may seem paradoxical with a nocturnal animal such as a leopard gecko, but remember that, either directly or indirectly, the sun provides leopard geckos with both light and heat. Modern reptile accessories make this a great deal easier than it used to be, but it is still more convenient to separate lighting from heating, and this is reflected in the commercially available products. This separation of these two key elements allows independent control where necessary.

Temperature

Leopard geckos are primarily thigmothermic (warm surface heat absorbers) and their heating requirements should reflect this. They have a preferred body temperature of around 28 to 30°C (82.4 to 86°F), but they can be exposed to widely differing temperatures in the wild, with some districts having an annual variation from 30°C (86°F) in the summer to –0.5°C (31.1°F) in the mid-winter.

Being nocturnal does not mean that they do not thermoregulate. It is likely that, given the choice, leopard geckos will choose retreats that allow them to maintain their body temperature at the correct level, without having to expose themselves. The rigours of their natural habitat means that leopard geckos actually appear to have quite a wide temperature tolerance, so there are several means of providing the correct thermal environment, depending upon the ambient room temperature. The various heating methods are not mutually exclusive and can be combined for optimum effect.

Always make sure your leopard gecko cannot directly touch any heat source, as burns can occur. The temperature beneath the basking light should be around 28 to 30°C (82.4 to 86°F), with a background temperature of around 20 to 25°C (68 to 77°F). A night-time fall is to be recommended and temperatures down to 18°C (64.4°F) are tolerated well.

1. In its simplest form heat can be provided by a spotlight or other tungsten or low wattage halogen bulb, which acts as a radiant heat source to mimic the sun. This provides daytime heat that will also warm the air in the vivarium. Ideally the bulb should be placed at one end of the vivarium so that a temperature gradient forms along the length of the vivarium to allow the Leopard Gecko to select the temperature it prefers. These lights should be connected to a thermostat so that the vivarium does not overheat, and to a timer so that the light is not for 24 hours a day, or worse still is perpetually flicking on and off as the thermostat reacts to the temperature.

2. Ceramic bulbs are available that only give out radiant heat and these are to be recommended because such bulbs can provide radiant heat throughout the day and night irrespective of the lighting regime. A less satisfactory alternative is a red bulb, which produces heat and only visible red light, and is less disturbing to the leopard geckos at night. Some people think that leopard geckos cannot see the colour red, but this is untrue; leopard geckos probably have good colour vision. There are also some blue bulbs available that emit light in the UVA spectrum.

3. Heat mats are also readily available and are often touted as a cheap and convenient means of supplying heat for leopard geckos. They are placed either under the vivarium or on the side to provide localised warm areas, but they are insufficient to warm a whole vivarium and generally are considered as supplementary heating only. They can help to produce warm microclimates under bark or similar. Having said that, many leopard geckos do manage to survive and thrive when only supplied with a heat mat.

This may be more feasible if the ambient temperature is reasonable, but I suspect that in many cases this probably reflects the versatility and hardiness of this gecko rather than any benefits of the system itself.

4. Hot rocks – imitation rocks with a heating element inside them - should be used with caution. Leopard geckos will rest on warm surfaces but if such 'hot rocks' are not thermostatically controlled then the risk of burning is increased. They are not strictly necessary and are probably best avoided.

Lighting

Leopard geckos are nocturnal, and so, their requirement for ultraviolet light exposure is likely to be less than diurnal reptiles.

It is true that they can be kept successfully without ultraviolet, providing sufficient dietary vitamin D3 is provided, indeed, if exposed to high levels of ultraviolet B light they will often hide away. leopard geckos do, however, benefit from low levels of ultraviolet B and those bulbs that emit 2.0% ultraviolet B are suitable. I have seen some cases of metabolic bone disease that did respond to low level ultraviolet B exposure. Ultraviolet light, just like other light wavelengths, can be reflected and it may be that even in the cracks and crevices where Leopard geckos spend the daytime hours, some ultraviolet light is reflected on to them by the surrounding surfaces. They may also bask at dusk and dawn.

The bulbs available provide artificial light for vivaria and typically it is provided by fluorescent tubing that has been tweaked to produce the important wavelengths of light for leopard geckos.

It also produces a light that renders more natural colouring and so appears like normal sunlight. These fluorescent tubes available to herpetologists emit light in the most important parts of the spectrum including UVB and UVA. Should you decide to use full spectrum lighting, there are some important points to remember:

1. Light intensity falls off inversely with distance from that light source so that if one doubles the distance between the leopard gecko and the light tube, the intensity of the light is halved. This is important as suspending a full spectrum light several feet above a leopard gecko will be of little use. The ideal distance will usually be supplied by the manufacturer, but if in doubt, suspend the tube around 30 to 45 cm above where the gecko rests.

2. Always position the bulb above the lizard. Leopard Geckos and other reptiles have eyebrow ridges designed to keep the eyes shaded from light from above. Lighting from the side, especially with high UVB levels, can cause serious eye problems.

3. Many of these lights are rated according to their UVB output, and this is indicated by a figure at the end of the trade name. Typically, these ratings are 2.0, 5.0, 8.0 and 10.0. Each figure refers to the percentage output of UVB and so a light rated as 2.0 should produce around 2% of its output as UVB. Leopard Geckos should have lights of no more than 2.0.

4. The shape of the tube affects the area of exposure to suitable levels of ultraviolet light. The compact tubes (which resemble economy light-bulbs in appearance) produce a fairly narrow beam of ultraviolet light, while the longer cylindrical fluorescent tubes emit a more even beam over the length of the tube. Ideally, the tubes should extend the full length of the vivarium, but if not, situate them close to the heat source so that the Leopard Gecko will be exposed to the beneficial lighting as it basks. Mesh tops can filter out up to 50% of the UV-B radiation; however this is unlikely to be a major issue for leopard geckos.

5. The lighting is best connected to a timer so that that the leopard gecko has a regular day: night pattern. I would suggest around 10 hour day to 14 hour night.

6. Always buy lights specifically designed for reptiles, as many fluorescents said to mimic the sun are colour-rendered to deceive our eyes and do not emit the correct spectrum. Unsuitable lights include those made for aquaria, general fluorescents available from hardware stores and ultraviolet tubes marketed for inclusion in pond filters. The latter are especially dangerous as they emit UV-C and can cause serious eye damage. Glass filters out UV light and so the correct tubes are made from quartz – which makes them more expensive than ordinary fluorescents. Price can therefore be a rough guide to your purchase.

7. Unfortunately, the UV output declines over time and these tubes do need replacing every eight to twelve months. Failure to do this can be a cause of metabolic bone disease in Leopard Geckos. In the past few years lighting that emits both the correct spectrum and heat have become available and work well. Combining the two obviously better mimics natural sunlight, but it does take away some of the flexibility inherent in having both functions separate. Always provide your Leopard Gecko with a hide of some sort so that it can retreat from the light should it want to.

Humidity, substrates & hygiene

Leopard geckos are from an arid environment and you might think that humidity is probably of little consequence, but you would be wrong. This is because the humidity levels found inside leopard geckos can be quite high. This is because the humidity levels found inside leopard gecko retreats can be quite high. Local humidity for correct skin shedding should be around 70 - 80 %.

Therefore, one should aim to provide localised areas where the humidity can be allowed to remain higher. Not only does this include such things as shedding boxes (see later) but even creating or buying commercially available hides. In addition, humidity can be temporarily enhanced, for example, when your gecko is shedding, by a combination of several means, including regular spraying with tepid water. Avoid excessive moisture because warm temperatures and high moisture levels can encourage a high environmental bacterial load.

Correct humidity is important for normal skin shedding.

Cleanliness therefore, becomes a serious issue within the leopard gecko vivarium, as it is in any relatively restricted enclosure. It is very tempting to try to set up naturalistic landscapes for leopard geckos, and they will benefit from them, but naturalistic vivaria are harder to keep clean because urine soaks readily into the substrate and faeces can be missed; there may even be a disincentive to remove soiled material in case it spoils the appearance. As discussed in the section on Natural History, leopard geckos create and utilize defaecatoriums. Such toilets can be used to our advantage. Once your leopard gecko has decided where his or her toilet will be, one can place an easily- moveable container or substrate in that place. 'Seed' the container with some faeces and this is likely to encourage the gecko to continue to use this area. One can then regularly remove the defaecatorium, clean it and return it without having to perform a major vivarium cleaning. Other than in the defaecatorium (where excessive cleanliness may cause your gecko to change its habits), always remove faeces when they are seen. Regular replacement of all the substrate will be required.

They may be small, but leopard geckos are predators.

There is no one ideal substrate for leopard geckos. Easily cleaned surfaces such as slate or paper will work well, but if you want to provide environmental enrichment consider using sand or a sand/soil mixture to encourage digging and foraging. Avoid larger gravels because these can be accidently ingested along with food. Too great a depth will inhibit the function of heat mats placed under the vivarium.

Sand is fine as a substrate, but avoid bark chippings (bottom) and similar.

Furniture

Furniture does not mean providing your Leopard gecko with a three-piece suite, but giving it things in its environment that make a leopard gecko home.

It will need places to hide and structures to climb on. Hides can be provided as rocks, pieces of bark, empty terracotta plant pots, commercially available imitation 'dens', often made to look like rocks, plastic and acrylic plants (of which there are now some very good examples) and large pieces of wood. Shelves placed on the back or sides of the vivarium will also increase the available space for your gecko to explore and exercise.

Unlike many other gecko species, leopard geckos are unable to climb vertical surfaces such as the glass sides, so surface area is important to them. However, rockwork (which if necessary should be stabilised) and branches will help to increase their available exercise area.

Other furniture that I would recommend is a shedding box. The idea is to provide a safe place with high humidity where your leopard gecko can shed its skin.

You can buy them ready-made or you can easily make one with a clean margarine tub. Cut a gecko-sized hole into the lid and fill the tub with a moisture-retentive substrate such as vermiculite or coir. If they are breeding, then an egg-laying box should be provided too, although in many cases a shedding container may double as a nesting area. And, of course, there should be a feed bowl and water bowl.

Give your geckos an environment worth living in.

Caring routine

Good husbandry of any pet involves establishing a certain routine and I would recommend that you buy a small notebook to keep a record of what you do. When cleaning food containers and vivarium structures always use a commercial reptile-safe disinfectant, available from good pet shops. Never use household disinfectants such as bleach. Always keep your reptile-cleaning equipment separate from your normal household materials.

Daily routine

- Check that the temperature and humidity readings are in correct range.

- Refresh drinking water.

- Offer food in line with the feeding recommendations outlined in Rules of Feeding at the end of the Nutrition section.

- A light spraying with a hand-held spray will help to raise humidity and encourage your gecko to drink. If possible do this in the morning, in part to mimic morning dew, but also to allow surfaces to dry and so avoid your lizard being exposed to a combination of cold and wet.

- Remove any obvious faeces as you see them.

- Change paper bedding if that is in use.

Weekly

- Thoroughly clean food and water containers.

- Clean glass doors.

- Search for and remove less obvious faecal material.

Monthly

- Thoroughly clean the inside of the vivarium making sure that you remove any faeces or urates from the vivarium furniture.

- Weigh your leopard gecko and log a record of its weight in your note book.

Regularly weigh your gecko to check its condition.

Six monthly to one year

- If you are using a full spectrum light, change it whether it appears fine or not (remember we humans cannot see ultraviolet light so we cannot tell if the bulbs are still emitting UV light just by looking). Make a note of the date in your diary or notebook.

- Replace the substrate.

Electrical safety

Keeping leopard geckos properly inevitably involves using electrical goods. Always use suitable products designed for keeping reptiles in accordance with the instructions supplied. If unsure consult a qualified electrician.

Nutrition

Nutrition

Adult leopard geckos are primarily
carnivores, eating any invertebrates,
such as insects and spiders, that
they are able to overpower. They are
active foragers rather than ambush
predators and will often test foods by
tongue-flicking them first. This brings
into use their vomerolfaction. They are
able to differentiate between potential
prey (swabs coated with cricket smell)
against palatable plant chemicals
(romaine lettuce) and control chemicals
(de-ionized water) [Cooper and
Habegger 2000].

In this study the leopard geckos increased tongue-
flicking when exposed to the cricket-swabs and
would even bite them, yet completely ignored the
others. This confirms leopard geckos as carnivores
and may explain why some, but by no means all, will
take dead insect prey.

Proteins and fats are the most important sources of energy for reptiles, with carbohydrates less so. Therefore in order to keep your leopard gecko healthy, a diet mimicking this should be offered. In practice leopard gecko foods can be divided into two groups: insects and commercial diets, although the latter are often based upon preserved insects.

Nutrient content of food

Food consists of a variety of different nutritional elements that need to be considered. These add up to the quality of any given food.

1. Good quality food provides what your leopard gecko requires whilst poor quality food is either deficient in some or all of these aspects, or else is inappropriate for the needs of the gecko.

2. Water is an essential part of the nutritional content of food. In addition to feeding the correct foods and regular misting, clean, free-standing water should always be available.

3. Protein is needed for growth and repair of the body. In leopard geckos, some is used as an energy source as well.

4. Fat is utilized reasonably well by leopard geckos, because of their insectivorous (and therefore carnivorous) nature.

Fat is needed especially by reproductively-active females, as most of the egg yolk consists of fatty materials which are an ideal store of energy for the developing embryo. Due to this, the types of fat consumed by female geckos may affect the viability of any eggs produced by her. Too high a fat diet can result in hepatic lipidosis.

5. Carbohydrates are a lesser energy source for leopard geckos. Primarily these are the simple sugars and starches produced by plants during photosynthesis.

6. Fibre is important in two main ways. First of all, part of it is digested by gut bacteria which break it down to smaller molecules that can be absorbed and used by the gecko. Secondly, its presence promotes normal gut motility and stool formation, both of which are vital to a normal gut environment.

7. Just like us, leopard geckos require a number of vitamins to remain healthy. Vitamins can broadly be divided into water-soluble and fat-soluble. The water-soluble vitamins such as vitamin C and the B vitamin group, cannot generally be stored and so need to be manufactured and used as needed.

Fat soluble vitamins on the other hand can be stored in the body's fat reserves. The most important fat soluble vitamin is vitamin D3. This is required to absorb calcium out of the gut and into the body. Without it, calcium cannot be taken up in significant quantities, even if a large amount is present in the food. It is produced in several stages. First of all provitamin D is converted to a second compound – previtamin D – in the skin under the presence of ultraviolet light. Previtamin D is then further converted to vitamin D3 by a second reaction, but this is a temperature dependant change and so the gecko must be at its preferred body temperature for this to happen. Vitamin D3 is then further converted into more active substances in both the liver and kidneys.

Vitamin D3 is of animal origin and when supplied as a dietary supplement is considered to be the only form of vitamin D that leopard geckos and other reptiles can utilise. This is important as some pet shop vitamin supplements contain vitamin D2 which is plant derived (and therefore cheaper), but will be of no use to the gecko.

Insects

A variety of insects are commercially available as live prey for pet reptiles. These include crickets, locusts, mealworms, silk worms, waxworms and phoenix worms. None of these insects are a complete diet in themselves and with the possible exception of phoenix worms, are significantly calcium deficient.

Their main advantage of live prey is that they move, which triggers predatory behaviour in your gecko. Some exercise is gained during the hunt and they certainly contribute to environmental enrichment. Sometimes leopard geckos can be trained to take non-moving food items such as dried insects, including commercially available dried mealworms, dried crickets, canned crickets and so on – a fact that can make their management much easier.

Crickets

Crickets are readily available in a variety of sizes from micro (hatchlings) at 2-4 mm up to adults at 25 – 30 mm. Several species are available including brown (Aheta domestica), banded (Gryllodes sigillatus) and black crickets (Gryllus bimaculatus). Nutritionally they are pretty much the same, although bandeds have slightly higher protein content (21% compared with around 15% for the other two). If crickets are not consumed quickly they can get hungry themselves and, on occasion, begin to feed on your gecko. Typically this occurs if too many crickets have been placed into the vivarium and the gecko cannot physically eat them all, or if the gecko is unwell and is not feeding. Always feed calcium supplemented crickets (see later). Crickets are also available in a dried form and canned, both of which are also occasionally taken by leopard geckos.

Locusts

Usually the species is Schistocera gregaria. Only the smaller locust nymphs (8 – 12 mm) are likely to be suitable for leopard geckos. These should be dusted and/or gut-loaded as for crickets. The same cares should be taken as with crickets.

Mealworms

Mealworms (Tenebrio molitor) are beetle larvae and are available in sizes from around 10 to 25 mm. With suitable supplements, mealworms can form a good basic diet for your gecko and are easily kept as they will not escape from a high-sided dish. Here they can be kept in a calcium-enriched powder until eaten. Many people have concerns about feeding mealworms to leopard geckos as there are horror stories of mealworms chewing their way back out, once eaten. In reality this is extremely unlikely to happen in a healthy leopard gecko, indeed their teeth appear to be eminently suitable for crushing hard-shelled prey. The adult beetles may also be eaten. Giant mealworms (Zophobas morio) are also suitable for adult leopard geckos. Mealworms are readily available in dried form, often as wild-bird food. These may be taken by leopard geckos, although some encouragement may be needed by artificially moving the prey item with forceps in front of the gecko, or using a vibrating feed bowl. When triggered remotely, this causes the mealworms to jiggle around. Once the lizard gets over its initially surprise (the mechanism is not silent) then feeding may be triggered. All mealworms, live or dried, should be dusted (or gut-loaded) as for crickets.

Waxworms

Waxworms (Galleria mellonella) are moth larvae
(the adults are actually a pest species found
in honey bee hives). They are quite fatty at
up to 25%. Over-feeding may risk obesity
in your gecko, but they are very useful
in feeding egg-laying females, which
transfer significant amounts of fat into
their eggs on a monthly basis. They also contain
the carotenoid pigments lutein and zeaxanthin.
Waxworms can be fed at all stages of their life-cycle
– pupae may be eaten as well as the adult moths.

Phoenix worms

These are the larvae of the black soldier fly Hermetia
illucens. Lengths range from a mere 1.5 mm up to 20
mm. They have an excellent calcium to phosphorus
ratio, even without calcium supplementation.

Dubia roaches

These cockroaches (Blaptica dubia) are becoming
increasingly available as live foods. They are
relatively high in protein and on a practical note are
not likely to develop into an embarrassing infestation
should they escape.

Silkworms

These are the caterpillars of the silkmoth. Small to medium (up to 3 cm) are suitable.

Canned foods are also available. These are made from various insects and other invertebrates such as earthworms and snails. At least one company markets a dried gecko food which consists of dried insect parts. Some leopard geckos may take these, but as often as not they are ignored.

Occasionally mice, in the form of neonatal mouse pups (pinkies) are recommended. Leopard geckos are not rodent predators and should not be offered these, except on a rare occasions, as they can cause obesity. The only source of calcium in a pinkie is the milk inside it's stomach because it's skeleton is made of cartilage, not bone.

Calcium supplements

Supplementing your leopard gecko's diet with calcium is vitally important. Most of the food items offered to leopard geckos are deficient in calcium (except phoenix worms). Remember that most of the commercially-available insects commonly fed to lizards are not produced because they are nutritionally good, but because they are easy to farm and they trigger normal feeding in insectivorous species.

Insects, because they have a chitinous exoskeleton, rather than a calcified endoskeleton, are a very poor source of calcium and so this must be balanced with commercial calcium supplements. These are applied to the insects either by dusting a calcium-rich powder on to the prey, or feeding them first upon a calcium-rich food. The latter is known as gut-loading. Many of the commercial calcium supplements also contain vitamins, including vitamin D3, as well as amino acids.

Young geckos which are growing rapidly, and reproductively active females, need calcium with every feed. Failure to do this will eventually lead to metabolic bone disease (see Leopard gecko Health).

Many leopard gecko keepers maintain a feed bowl with crushed cuttlefish or calcium carbonate powder in the vivarium. Leopard geckos will help themselves to these sources of calcium, and it is especially important to offer this to breeding females. This supply of calcium is in addition to, and not as an alternative to, food supplementation.

Calcium is needed for healthy bones.

Water

A shallow bowl, dish or water feature, containing clean water, should always be available. Leopard geckos will also drink water droplets from a hand-spray.

Rules of feeding

1. Clean drinking water should always be available.

2. Offer live food daily or every other day.

3. Never leave live crickets or locusts in the vivarium for longer than one day. Count them in, and count them out again (minus those that have been eaten, of course). Mealworms can be left in a bowl of calcium-supplemented powder until consumed.

4. The length of the largest cricket should be no greater than the width between the eyes of your gecko.

5. Geckos will happily survive for a week without feeding, so should you go on a short holiday, feed them well for a week or two before you go, then leave them to it. Someone should check them on a regular basis, however, in case of problems.

References

Cooper W.E. and Habegger J.J. (2000) Lingual and Biting Responses to Food Chemicals by Some Eublepharid and Gekkonid Geckos. Journal of Herpetology, Vol. 34, No. 3. pp. 360-368.

Reproduction

Sexual maturity in leopard geckos, like all reptiles, is dependant upon it reaching a certain size and weight, rather than age. Therefore sexual maturity is usually at a snout-vent length of around 9.0 cm and at a weight of around 30 g (males) or 35 g (females).

In males, maturity can be as early as five months old if the geckos are well fed, and ten months for females, or as long as 12 months if conditions are poorer. Once a snout-vent length of around 8 to 9 cm is reached, hemipenal bulges will begin to develop in the males. Previously described, this is probably the most accurate way to sex sexually mature leopard geckos. High temperature incubated females, with their heightened aggression and male appearance, never develop hemipenes. Adult males are often heavier than females and appear 'chunkier', with a thicker-set body. Females should weigh at least 35 to 40 g, preferably more, before being mated. Smaller males may be sexually mature, but may not be physically able, or allowed to, mate with larger females.

Males often have a broader, heavier head (upper gecko) than females (lower).

Sexual behaviour

Female leopard geckos will breed roughly every month for some eight or nine months of the year, resting for the remainder. This rest period is to be encouraged and has probably evolved to coincide with the cooler seasons experienced in their natural range. Dropping the temperature to around 18 to 23°C (64.4 to 73.4°F) should help to discourage mating, although many leopard geckos will stop during the northern hemisphere winter period without altering their environment.

Mating, as with most things in a leopard gecko's life, tends to occur during the hours of darkness, although it can be seen at any time of the day or night. Courtship behaviour is described elsewhere. Leopard geckos do not appear to form bonded pairings, so a reproductively active female in the wild would be likely to have several suitors. Indeed, it seems that females that mate with several males produce more clutches of eggs (and therefore more eggs) and more of these will be fertile (LaDage 2007).

Actual copulation lasts for two to three minutes. The male will climb on to the back of the female, grasp her neck or shoulder tightly in his mouth, whilst manoeuvring his pelvis to one side of her tail, so that he can insert one or other of his hemipenes into her cloaca for a successful mating. This biting can leave superficial wounds on the female and if necessary these can be cleaned with salt water or a dilute iodine solution.

Occasionally after mating the hemipene of the male will not retract immediately. He will usually clean it himself with his tongue and it should retract within a few hours. If it does not then consult a veterinarian as it may need to be either replaced, or if badly traumatised, amputated.

Egg production can be quite a drain on a female's body resources. Fat is mobilised from stores such as the abdominal fat pads and carried to the ovaries where it forms part of the yolk, which has to nourish the developing embryo until after its post-hatching shed when it can begin to feed. The shells of leopard gecko eggs are quite calcified, and this calcium, which is the last layer to be placed around the contents of the egg, is drawn directly from the skeleton of the mother and needs to be replenished from her food intake.

Practical breeding

Breeding leopard geckos can be maintained in pairs or small groups of one male to 2 to 5 females. This can be in a normal vivarium or in a more clinical set-up with paper substrate and hides made of either disposable materials, such as cardboard egg-cartons, or those that are easily cleaned such as half plant pots, so as to provide multiple hiding and resting places.

Such set-ups have the advantage of being easy to clean and the geckos are encouraged to lay in an egg-laying box provided, making egg collection easy. These arrangements make it ideal for commercial breeders, but for the home hobbyist, who wants to give his geckos a more natural vivarium and the environmental enrichment that that entails, it is not really suitable.

In addition to the usual equipment and arrangements, a breeding vivarium should contain an egg-laying box and a ready source of calcium. The first can be constructed along the same lines as the shedding box previously described. Again, a clean margarine or other plastic tub (around 7 to 10 cm deep) is used and a hole is cut into the lid just large enough for the female to be able to access. Fill it to around half deep with a moisture-retentive substrate such as vermiculite and add just enough water to make it feel damp, but not soggy. There is one report of suspected vermiculite poisoning in a breeding leopard gecko that had eaten a significant amount. This one account should be weighed against the countless thousands of geckos (and other reptiles) that are offered vermiculite as an egg deposition substrate with no problems at all. Some females will happily lay up to ten clutches in the same container, before the medium needs changing.

However, it is probably best to change the egg-laying substrate after every clutch as some females will only use it once and will try to select another place (often beneath or next to it) to lay their next if it is not 'fresh'. A small dish containing a source of calcium, such as a commercially available calcium carbonate powder, should be provided for the females. This is in addition to, and not instead of, normal calcium supplementation.

Preparation for breeding in leopard geckos should begin during their reproductively dormant period. If you have the space, then males should be separated from the females, but this is not essential. Make sure that the geckos are well fed and that plenty of calcium is supplied.

Leopard geckos can lay a clutch of two eggs as often as every 15 to 20 days if well fed, or as infrequently as 38 to 42 days, for some four to six months of the year. Young females may only lay one egg for their first and even second attempt. There is no real parental care from either parent. Gravid females will therefore look to lay their eggs in a place they feel is suitable for incubation. They will chose a spot based upon the following criteria:

- Temperature. The female will want an incubation medium at a suitable temperature for incubation, typically around 25 to 33°C (77 to 91.4°F).

- Moisture. The embryo will absorb water from its surroundings as it grows; if the substrate is too dry then the egg and embryo will dehydrate; if too wet then the embryo may drown or bacterial and fungal infections could challenge the developing egg.

- The mother wants to feel that her eggs will avoid predation, so she will choose a site with a reasonable depth of substrate, often in a confined space.

A low temperature incubated albino.

All of the above is why egg-laying boxes are so useful. The lid with an entrance hole not only gives a feeling of security, it also helps to maintain a localised humid atmosphere and reduces the rate of substrate drying. If the temperature is correct and the substrate clean and appropriately moist, then most females will choose to use them.

In females close to egg-laying, the eggs can, with practice, often be seen as two large, firm oval-sized objects in the back half of the body cavity. They can also be palpated, but this must be done very gently, because excessive pressure could rupture the eggs, which would trigger a massive internal reaction. If you can see or feel the eggs, then you know that the female is due to lay and you can keep a closer watch on her.

Occasionally, in larger naturalistic vivaria, egg-laying will be missed or the egg-laying box will be ignored and the clutch deposited somewhere else. If conditions are right these eggs may incubate and hatch, giving you a very pleasant surprise when a hatchling is unexpectedly found. These should be removed as soon as seen, because adult leopard geckos can be cannibalistic to hatchlings.

Egg laying

Egg deposition occurs at night. The female will dig a suitable hole at her chosen spot with her hind legs. As she pushes the egg out, her back feet help to guide it into the hole she has made. Once both eggs are laid she will cover the eggs as best she can and will eventually leave them to their fate.

Incubation

Temperature-dependent sex determination

Temperature Dependent Sex Determination (TDSD) occurs in leopard geckos. This is discussed in detail elsewhere, but the table below is presented as a recap.

TEMPERATURE °C	SEX RATIO (%) MALES: FEMALES
26	0 : 100
30	30 : 70
32.5	70 : 30
34	0 : 100 (approx)

Practical incubation

Leopard gecko eggs, unlike bird eggs, do not need to be turned, so this makes making an incubator relatively straight forward. Commercial reptile incubators and incubator kits are available, but, should you wish to make your own, any heat resistant container will do. You obviously need a heat source, which can be a small light bulb, a ceramic heater or a vivarium heat mat, connected to an accurate thermostat, which has a temperature probe that can be laid next to the eggs. An accurate thermometer is also required, and ideally a hygrometer to measure humidity should be used. The incubator must not be permanently sealed as some air exchange is necessary, even if this is only by lifting the lid once daily to check on the eggs.

The eggs do not need to be buried. Use a small container such as an old clean margarine tub and place some perlite as a substrate into this tub. Then place each egg on to the perlite in such a way as to create a shallow depression. The eggs should not be touching. Place a card or other label with the species and date of lay in the same tub.

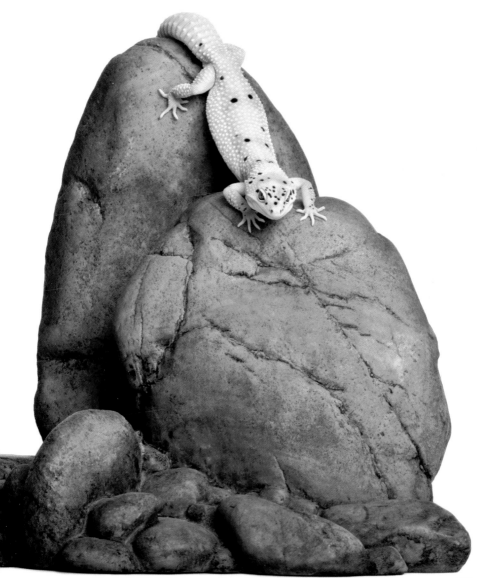

Temperature is crucial for normal development as is humidity. Adjust the temperature according to what sex you wish the young to be (see previous page) and for a humidity of 80 - 95%. To achieve these high humidity levels, soak the perlite with roughly the same weight of clean, warm water, then drain off any excess, before placing it in the nest box. The perlite should be damp, but not soaking wet. Do not spray the eggs to keep the humidity high – instead, add water in small amounts to the incubation media.

An alternative method of incubation is to dispense with substrate altogether and rest the eggs directly on to a plastic mesh suspended over a water resevoir maintained at the correct temperature. A plastic egg crate light diffuser is ideal for this. The eggs are therefore incubated in a highly humid environment, but have no water touching them directly.

Incubation periods

The incubation length can vary considerably depending upon the temperature of incubation (lower temperatures produce longer incubation times). At 27°C (80.6°F) it is around 60 days. At the high temperature end, incubation can be as short as 45 days, while at lower temperatures it can extend to 100 or so days. Prolonged temperatures below 24°C (75.2°F) are likely to cause embryonic death, as are temperatures above 35°C (95°F).

In some cases an egg within a clutch may exhibit diapause, where some eggs show a temporary halt in development, often at the early stages. This may be an adaptive process to stagger the hatching of young over a period of time, possibly to reduce the risk of exposing all of a given brood to unfavorable environmental conditions. There, some pairs of eggs will hatch within a few hours of each other, while others may be many days apart.

Apparent infertility

Adult leopard geckos may be infertile for a variety of reasons, but sometimes their eggs do not develop because the nutrition of the adults is poor. It is wise therefore, to offer a varied diet with appropriate supplements as detailed in the nutrition chapter.

Failure to hatch/dead-in-shell

There are many reasons why gecko eggs do not hatch. In the first instance consider the following:

1. Temperature. Temperatures too high or too low can lead to embryonic death

2. Humidity must be monitored and, if possible, a humidity of 80 - 95% maintained. A very low humidity or a high airflow over the eggs can lead to an excessive loss of water from the eggs, leading to dehydration and embryonic death. An egg that loses 25% or more of its weight during incubation is unlikely to hatch.

3. Oxygen and carbon dioxide levels. Remember that a developing Leopard Gecko inside the egg does breathe, not through its lungs, but across the egg shell. On the inside of the shell are membranes well supplied with blood vessels that pick up oxygen through microscopic holes in the shell and disperse carbon dioxide the same way.

In sealed incubators or containers housed inside larger incubators, oxygen levels may fall and carbon dioxide levels rise to dangerous levels. Briefly opening such incubators once daily or every other day will prevent this from happening.

Once an egg is laid and has come to rest, the embryo (which at this stage consists of only an aggregate of cells), gradually migrates up to the highest point of the shell so that it eventually comes to sit on top of the yolk. After 24 to 48 hours it attaches to the inner cell membrane - the allantois. This membrane is important for oxygen uptake and carbon dioxide release, calcium absorption from the shell and storage of harmful waste products. This connection is essential but is, to start with, very fragile. Any rotation of the egg within the period of 24 hours after laying to around 20 days of incubation is liable to sheer off the embryo and cause its subsequent death.

When handling eggs always be careful not to rotate them. When removing eggs from natural egg sites, to place into incubators, always try to do it within 24 hours of laying and mark the top of each egg with a permanent marker pen or similar so that you always know which way is up.

Fertile eggs increase in size as the embryo develops and this can be one way of deciding whether your eggs are fertile or not. Another is by candling. This involves shining a very bright light through the egg. If there is a sizable embryo present it will be seen as a shadow, and sometimes the blood vessels lining the inside of the shell can be picked up earlier in incubation. However, a shadow is often not visible until almost the end of incubation – possibly because it is only by this point that the developing gecko is dense enough to block any light. Do not rotate the egg while handling it.

Hatching

As incubation progresses the shell becomes thinner in patches as calcium is absorbed from the outer calcified layer and incorporated into the developing hatchling. Eventually, the gecko will hatch. There are two small "egg teeth" at the front of the upper jaw of the hatchling gecko, and it uses these to wear its way through the shell, creating a slit in the shell. Often once the shell is punctured and a small slit made, the gecko may take a rest.

Eventually, the hatchling will be able to climb out of the shell, physically a perfect miniature of the adult. The appearance of the hatchling will depend to some extent on which morph it is, but usually they are banded with yellow and black or mauve bars. They may have pink or bluish tinges. The tubercles start to become apparent after one week and as they grow and mature the barring and blotches gradually change into the adult pattern.

Occasionally, some hatching geckos will appear to have trouble getting out of their shell. It is tempting to help them, but be careful, hatchlings often have large yolk sacs still that have not been absorbed, and the blood vessels lining the inside of the shell are still functional. It is very easy to damage these structures with a serious risk of haemorrhage or wounding.

Rearing your own leopard geckos is very satisfying and educational.

Rearing

These newly hatched leopard geckos still have a yolk sac internally to supply them with food for the first few days, and usually will not begin to feed until after their first post-hatching skin shed (at around three days old). This shed is normally eaten and may not be seen. At three days onward you can offer them supplemented small mealworms or tiny crickets, as discussed in Nutrition.

Hatchling geckos can spend their first few days in the incubator before being transferred to a vivarium. These babies may gape and emit a screeching sound as a threat display! It looks cute, but remember they do this because they think that you are a potential predator.

Ideally, keep your newly hatched leopard gecko separate (or with its clutch-mate) in a small vivarium – the small acrylic pet carriers are ideal, until you are happy that it is eating. Once you see faeces then you know that your new gecko is eating and digesting properly and it can then be upgraded to a more naturalistic home. Do not place hatchlings back in with the adults as they may be eaten.

Close to egg-laying, the eggs will be (gently) palpable, and may be visible, in the abdominal area.

The husbandry advice discussed under *leopard gecko care* should be implemented, but of particular importance is the provision of hiding places. Hatchling and young leopard geckos have many predators in the wild and so instinctively they appreciate cover, behaviour that will also lead them into appropriate micro-climates that help them to survive. This is especially the case if several babies are kept in the same vivarium. Humidity is also important, as leopard gecko hatchlings are very susceptible to shedding problems and can easily lose toes from tourniquets of dried skin around their digits.

Selective breeding & genetics

Much of the interest in leopard geckos is centred around the widely different colour morphs that are available and because of this there is a great deal of interest in selective breeding to stabilise, reproduce and improve on these. Repeated close crossings can cause problems with reduced fertility and the inadvertent selection for bad characteristics, such as underlying heart disease (as is seen in some breeds of dogs).

References

LaDage, L.P. (2007) The socio-sexual behaviors of the Leopard Gecko (Eublepharis macularius) Dissertation. The University of Memphis, 2007, 91 pages; AAT 3276716

Health

Health

If kept and fed properly, leopard geckos are surprisingly trouble free. Many of the conditions that we do see in them can be traced back to poor management practices and therefore can, with some forethought, be avoided.

Leopard geckos that are ill are best kept in vivaria where their environment can be controlled appropriately. Ideally, use only newspaper or paper toweling on the floor so that it can be cleaned out readily, and make sure that any vivarium furniture, such as hides and bowls, can either be sterilised or thrown away. Basic care for an unwell leopard gecko should also include the following:

- Provision of a stress-free environment.

- Provide an appropriate temperature of around 28 to 30°C (82.4 to 86°F). If kept at too low a temperature a gecko's immune system will not function correctly.

Equally, if the gecko is on medication, such as antibiotics, keeping it at its preferred body temperature will mean that its body manages and eliminates the drug in a manner predictable to your veterinary surgeon.

- Weigh your leopard gecko on scales that weigh to the nearest 1g. This can be done monthly if your gecko is well, or as frequently as daily if necessary. This information will be useful to your veterinarian.

- Keeping the gecko well hydrated is essential. Many leopard geckos will lick water gently applied to their mouths with a syringe or dropper. Spray the vivarium daily to maintain humidity and create further drinking opportunities.

- If you have concerns it is best to arrange a consultation with your veterinarian so that your leopard gecko can be examined and its problems analysed and dealt with professionally.

Metabolic bone disease

Bone diseases can be common in lizards of all species, and any limb swelling, fracture or paralysis should be considered as a possible sign of an underlying bone disorder. Metabolic Bone Disease (MBD) is actually a group of skeletal disorders that are largely – but not exclusively – dietary related. Common causes include a dietary calcium deficiency, a dietary calcium/phosphorus imbalance, a dietary vitamin D3 deficiency, lack of exposure to ultra violet light, dietary protein deficiency or excess, and liver, kidney or intestinal disease.

Signs of MBD include weakness, loss of appetite and swollen limbs. Closer examination may reveal that the jaws are extremely soft and can be easily deformed (please test this gently as it likely to be painful for the gecko). Excessive handling may trigger autotomy. In females, eggs may be palpable in the body cavity and indeed this may be the final straw. Female geckos that have marginal calcium levels may go into a sudden calcium crash by mobilizing what little calcium they do have into their egg shells prior to laying.

Most skeletal problems in leopard geckos are dietary linked and should a gecko start to manifest such signs then you should immediately consider the following:

1. Diet. Consider increasing or improving the calcium content of the diet by dusting and/or gut loading prey.

2. Lighting. Make sure there is provision for ultraviolet lighting. Leopard geckos can be kept without full spectrum lighting, but to compensate they must have dietary vitamin D3, usually combined with good calcium supplement. A daytime full spectrum bulb with a 2% ultraviolet output can be beneficial, allowing the gecko to bask if it wants to. Always check that the light positioning is appropriate (usually around 30 cm above the animal) close to a heat source (to encourage basking) and that they are changed regularly (every eight to twelve months). Ultraviolet outputs greater than 2% are unnecessary and will probably just result in your gecko hiding away.

3. If the gecko shows severe signs or is lethargic or anorexic then seek veterinary advice, as secondary infections are common in such animals. Your leopard gecko may need radiography, blood tests or other tests to establish what is causing the problem. Treatments can include injecting vitamin D3, injecting calcium, plus dealing with other underlying causes, such as liver disease.

Parasites

Cryptosporidium

This is a serious protozoan (single-celled) parasite of leopard geckos that has become a real scourge. Cryptosporidum saurophilum appears to be specific to lizards and the leopard gecko seems to be particularly susceptible to it. The main problem that the parasite causes is a gross thickening of the large bowel, which appears to affect the gecko's ability to absorb its food. What we see is a progressive loss of condition of the gecko, even though the gecko is, at least initially, bright and alert and still feeding. Eventually, these geckos become skeletally thin, go off their food and die. It is a very difficult condition to treat and there is, at the time of writing, no reliable cure. Some antibiotics help, and feeding probiotics may also help an infected leopard gecko to recover, but this is by no means certain. The risk of crytosporididosis is one of the main reasons why one should only purchase your gecko from a reputable supplier.

Flagellates

Flagellates are single-celled parasites that regularly cause gut-problems, weight loss and loss of appetite in leopard geckos. The gecko's faeces will be very runny, and if you put some under a medium power light microscope, huge numbers of mobile, pear-shaped protozoa will be seen. They are often a secondary problem, often appearing in such large numbers often when something else (such as cryptosporidiosis or poor standards of care) is suppressing the gecko's immune system. Consult your veterinarian as they are easily treated with metronidazole.

Oxyurid nematodes

Oxyurid nematodes are small intestinal worms that are common in pet lizards, but rarely cause serious problems. You are unlikely to see any worms in the faeces – their presence is usually given away by spotting their eggs on microscopic examination of droppings. They do compete with the gecko for the food that it eats and heavy burdens may cause weight loss, while lighter infestations may have more subtle effects such as poorer growth rate and fertility. The life cycle of oxyurids is direct and control is by worming with appropriate wormers, such as fenbendazole, available from your veterinarian, and by regular removal of faeces.

Autotomy

The loss of the tail is not a disease, but does occasionally happen. Keep the stump clean, for example, with a very dilute iodine solution, and allow it to heal naturally. A new tail will eventually grow. If the raw stump is surgically repaired, then a new tail will not form.

Abnormal skin shedding

Normal skin shedding is properly termed ecdysis – abnormal or problematic shedding is called dysecdysis. This can appear as patches of dull, thickened skin that may indicate areas where several layers of skin have built up over successive dysecdysis episodes. Rings of unshed skin may form bands around the tips of extremities such as toes and tail tips. These may constrict as they dry, acting as tourniquets and compromising blood flow to the extremities. leopard geckos that have had previous problems may lack one or more digits. Such bands of tight skin need to be removed. Moisten the affected areas with a damp cotton bud in order to loosen the retained skin from the underlying epidermis. Occasionally, retained shed skin will seal the eyelids together. These should be gently prized open with a damp cotton bud. In leopard geckos dysecdysis is commonly associated with low humidity levels and is especially a problem with hatchlings and young geckos.

Eye problems

Eye problems do seem to be an issue with leopard geckos. Sometimes it can be due to particles of sand or other substrate getting trapped in the eye, sometimes they are linked with a poor skin shed, while other times it appears to be an infection. Typically, the eyelids are swollen shut, and one or both eyes may be affected. Gently washing with a damp cotton bud may be beneficial to help open the eye. Occasionally, there is a build-up of thick pus-like material behind the eyelids (this can make it look as though there is no eye present!). This material needs to be removed – consult your veterinarian as the eye is easily and irreparably damaged in unskilled hands, and follow-up antibiotic treatment may be necessary.

Gut impactions

Gut impactions or blockages are often linked to substrate types. Small bark chippings or pea gravel are the worst offenders, but sand will impact. I have even seen impactions with sands made of allegedly digestible calcium carbonate. Usually it occurs after pieces of substrate are inadvertently picked up and ingested during feeding, although it may be intentional in those geckos with mineral deficits such as breeding females, or occasionally in diseases that create a disturbed appetite.

The beautiful and intricate iris of a healthy leopard gecko.

You may be able to actually feel the impaction (please be gentle if trying this), but X-rays will be needed to assess the type of impaction, and eliminate other underlying problems e.g. pelvic problems. Bark, however, will not show on X-rays.

To treat, make sure that the gecko is well hydrated and you can try lubricants such as liquid paraffin, but some may require surgery so consult your veterinarian.

Egg-binding

Any adult female leopard gecko that shows non-specific signs of ill health, restlessness or persistent straining should be assessed for egg-binding (dystocia). There are two forms:

1. Pre-ovulatory Ovarian Stasis. The eggs grow in the ovaries but are not ovulated, so the ovaries become overloaded with retained yolks. This appears to be rare in Leopard Geckos.

2. Post-ovulatory. Here eggs that are shelled to varying degrees are present within the oviducts. It is easily diagnosed by radiography, as the shells show up easily. There are many possible causes for this, including environmental (no provision of suitable egg deposition sites), low calcium levels, fractured or deformed pelvis, internal tumours and so on, so your veterinarian may need to do several tests to investigate this.

Treatment involves providing the correct environment, including appropriate temperature, humidity and nesting chamber, and this may induce normal egg-laying. Supplement well with calcium. If this fails then you will need to take your gecko to a veterinarian, who may consider medical induction with calcium and oxytocin or percutaneous ovocentesis. In this case the egg contents are sucked out by syringe through a needle inserted through the body wall so that the shrunken eggs can be passed. This must be done under general anaesthesia. Surgical removal (a caesarian) is another option.

Finally, some general points on salmonellosis in reptiles. These bacteria are probably best considered as a normal constituent of lizard cloacal/gut microflora. They are rarely pathogenic to lizards, but excretion is likely to increase during times of stress e.g. movement or illness. In reality, to healthy hobbyists the risk is minimal and infections in reptile owners are very rare. If isolated, treatment is usually not appropriate as it is unlikely to be effective long-term and may encourage antibiotic resistance.

Recommendations for prevention of salmonellosis from captive reptiles issued by the Center for Disease Control in the USA are:

1. Pregnant women, children less than five years of age and persons with impaired immune system function (e.g. AIDS) should not have contact with reptiles.

2. Due to the risk of becoming infected with Salmonella from a reptile, even without direct contact, households with pregnant women, children under five years of age or persons with impaired immune system function should not keep reptiles. Reptiles are not appropriate pets for childcare centres.

3. All persons should wash hands with soap immediately after any contact with a reptile or reptile cage.

4. Reptiles should be kept out of food preparation areas such as kitchens.

5. Kitchen sinks should not be used to wash food or water bowls, cages or vivaria used for reptiles, or to bath reptiles. Any sink used for these purposes should be disinfected after use.

Acknowledgement

Thank you to David Davies of Welsh Reptile Breeders for his helpful comments on this manuscript.

Weights & measures

If you prefer your units in pounds and inches, you can use this conversion chart:

Length in inches	Length in cm	Weight in kg	Weight in lbs
1	2.5	0.5	1.1
2	5.1	0.7	1.5
3	7.6	1	2.2
4	10.2	1.5	3.3
5	12.7	2	4.4
8	20.3	3	6.6
10	25.4	4	8.8
15	38.1	5	11

Measurements rounded to 1 decimal place.